LORI HUGHES

INNER GAME OF STRESS

The Ultimate Guide on Coping With Stress, Learn How Effective Methods to Eliminate Stress So You Can Think With a Clear Mind

Descrierea CIP a Bibliotecii Naționale a României
LORI HUGHES
   INNER GAME OF STRESS. The Ultimate Guide on Coping With Stress, Learn How Effective Methods to Eliminate Stress So You Can Think With a Clear Mind / Lori Hughes – Bucharest: Editura My Ebook, 2021
   ISBN

LORI HUGHES

INNER GAME OF STRESS

The Ultimate Guide on Coping With Stress, Learn How Effective Methods to Eliminate Stress So You Can Think With a Clear Mind

My Ebook Publishing House
Bucharest, 2021

TABLE OF CONTENTS

FOREWORD

This *is* an eBook that gives you an insight on how you can abolish stress from your life. Stress is the number cause for unhappiness. It makes one live a very unsatisfying life. In addition, research shows that there are so many illnesses that occur as a result of being stressed.

In this eBook, you will get to learn more about. This includes what it means and how it affects a person. There are so many people who are undergoing stress but they don't even know it.

In addition, you will learn some of the symptoms of stress. This will help you in identifying stress in advance and being able to get rid of it before it gets worse.

There is a general assumption that stress is a bad thing. Many people thinks of it as frustrating and bringing about feelings of discomfort and general unhappiness. However, not all stress is bad.

There is a category of stress that is actually highly recommended for every person. In this eBook, you will learn about the different types of stress and how they occur. Try and establish which kind of stress you are going through or are likely to go through in future.

In this eBook, you will also learn what exactly causes stress. This will help you in identifying areas in your life that are likely to bring you stress. If you are currently feeling stressed, you may be able to point out the stressor. It is very important to know what is stressing you. This is the only way that you can manage to get rid of the stressor.

Stress normally has very negative effects on individuals. It can affect one's mind and also body. It can also affect the people around. Stress generally affects an individual's ability to be happy and live a quality life.

In this eBook, you will learn about the effects that stress has on you. This will give you good reasons as to why you have to abolish stress in life immediately. You may be surprised to know just how much your life has been affected by stress.

It is possible to abolish stress from your life. No matter how bad things may seem right now. You can get rid of stress. This will enable you to enjoy your life better. It will also help in improving your mental and physical health. You just have to make a few changes in your life and you will be able to live a stress-free life. In this eBook, you will get some good tips on how to abolish stress. You can use this tips for your own situations or even give them to someone else who is having a hard time in their lives.

If you aren't stressed out, you can learn how to stay this way. It is possible to avoid being stressed and keep living a good satisfying life. These tips can also help people who have managed to abolish stress in their lives. It will give them tips to avoid getting stressed again. In this eBook, you will learn how to stay away from stress.

There are times when individuals are convinced that things will never get better. For instance, a person going through tough times like a bad divorce maybe so stressed out. This stress may last just a few months until the person adjusts to being single again. However, this stress may also be chronic. There are people who spend most part of their lives being stressed. This definitely robs them of the opportunity to live a good quality life. This eBook is meant to give readers tips on how to get control of their lives. It tells them how they can live life without ever being stressed out.

This eBook is written in very easy English that can easily be understood. This simplicity makes it very fascinating and at the same time informative. You will benefit a lot from reading this book. By the time, you put it down; you will have learnt how to get rid of stress in your life. If you apply the tips given, this will be the start of a good stress-free life for you.

Stress Soothers

Abolish Stress From Your System And Think
With A Clear Mind

CHAPTER 1

AN OVERVIEW OF STRESS

Synopsis

Every day in our life has factors and events that can be stressful. We are constantly surrounded by stressors. In this chapter, you will learn more about stress. This will give you a deeper understanding of this issue.

➤ What does it mean to be stressed?

➤ What brings about stress?

➤ How can I know that I am stressed?

If you are constantly ill, unhappy or feeling frustrated, you could be stressed. Stress can occur even when you least expect it. Understanding this issue will help you know to avoid it or abolish it from your life.

Stress

Life is so full of ups and downs which make it very difficult for a person to always be upbeat all the time. There are events or circumstances that can make one feel overwhelmed or stressed out. All areas of life present opportunities of stress. However, not all stress is bad. There is stress that is normally good. It helps one to get motivated and better prepared to effectively handle different tasks.

Stress may easily occur if a person is pushing themselves too bad. It doesn't matter whether they are doing this mentally or physically. The strain can bring about a feeling an unhappiness and of being overwhelmed by responsibilities. People who find they are not getting enough rest due to any given factors are very likely to be stressed.

12

Pushing yourself too hard can cause you to breakdown in stress.

To avoid getting overwhelmed by stress, you need to learn the symptoms that can alert you about being stressed out. These symptoms will alert you that you need to take action to alleviate the stress in your life. You also need to learn how stress occurs. This will help you learn how to avoid stressful situations. There are many people who are living with stress; they have come to accept this as the norm. However, this is very dangerous. Stress can harm a person and greatly have a negative impact on the quality of their lives.

Understanding stress

Stress signals are normally send to the brain by the nervous system. These signals may be as a result of a stressor such as fear or even a threat. These signals alert the brain that something is amiss. These signals or hormones will then be transmitted to the body. They will present themselves in form of high blood pressure, rapid heartbeat rate and breathing, tightening of muscles and heightened alertness.

Stress can easily occur at anytime, sometimes you may not even be able to tell when a stressor is about to happen. For instance, receiving bad news such as the death of a loved one can be very stressful. This may happen unexpectedly and therefore cause you instant acute stress.

This is the body's way of responding to the event. You may also get a threat that can get you stressed out. The threat may be real or even perceived. However, your body will naturally react to this, telling you something is amiss. This is commonly referred to as the, stress response.

Stress response is not necessarily a bad thing. Sometimes it helps a person stay upbeat about life. It can also help a person to get motivated and give their best performance in a given task. It can also help a person to get their defences up in case of danger. For instance, when being attacked a person will be able to react faster and get themselves away from the attacker. However, this only happens when it is working well. Negative stress response works in the opposite. It can get a person feeling very down and overwhelmed by life.

You always have to keep your stress levels in check. If you let the stress overwhelm you then this can definitely be dangerous. Sometimes, stress can get into your life without you even realizing it. You will only be aware of it when things get out of hand. In other instances, it can get into your life and without realizing it you accept it and therefore make it part of your daily routine. This is how people end up living with chronic stress for a lifetime.

Common responses to stress

Stress can get someone on edge. There are people who react to stress by being very angry. They will be overly frustrated to the point of being unable to do anything else. This will affect how they relate to their family members and even to their friends and colleagues. This people will seem highly irritable and sensitivity. They will have a very strong emotional reaction even with just a little provocation.

One of the most common responses to stress is angry outbursts.

There are also people who react to stress by becoming very withdrawn. This is sometimes referred to as, "feeling down". A person will no longer be excited about anything in their lives.

They may even stop doing the things that they used to previously enjoy. Such a person may appear to be sad and gloomy. They will not open up about their problems and instead they may actually alienate themselves from other people.

Other people react to stress seemingly very calmly on the surface. They may seem quiet and not really doing anything out of the ordinary. However, inside there is no calmness. This is like a combination of the above two responses. They shut down and at the same time, experience turmoil internally. Their minds may be restless although this may not show in their actions.

Symptoms of Stress Psychological Symptoms

These may include forgetfulness. It may also include the inability to concentrate on any given task even for a short period of time. A person may also start making irrational judgement and poor choices in life. This can happen to even the people who normally appear to be very level headed. A person may also appear to be constantly worrying and sad. They will have a very negative attitude and may be pessimistic about life. This person will also be constantly in thought. The mind will not be getting much rest due to the racing thoughts.

Emotional Symptoms

Stress will also affect person's emotions. They may start having regular mood swings, being quick tempered and very irritable. They may also be constantly agitated and un-relaxed. A person will start feeling overwhelmed by life and their responsibilities. This person may also start feeling lonely even if they aren't. They will also feel like other people have alienated them. A stressed person will be very unhappy. They are also likely to be depressed.

Being constantly irritable can be a symptom that you are stressed out.

Physical symptoms

Stress usually takes a toll on someone's body. Some of the likely physical symptoms include random or chronic pains and aches. It can also bring about frequent common colds. A person may also have constipations and diarrhoea. They are also likely to experience dizziness and nausea. Stress can also make the heart beat much faster and make someone experience some chest pains. Stress makes a person lose interest in sex.

Behavioural symptoms

Stress will definitely bring changes in a person's behaviours. It may make them loose or gain appetite. It can also bring about insomnia although other people tend to sleep a lot when stressed. A person may consciously or unconsciously start isolating themselves from others. Stress may make a person start neglecting their responsibilities either at work or even at home.

A person may also turn to drugs, alcohol or cigarette smoking as an escapism strategy. Stress can also cause nervousness and anxiety making a person paranoid or unable to sit still.

CHAPTER 2

AN OVERVIEW OF DIFFERENT TYPES OF STRESS

Synopsis

In this chapter, we look at the different categories of stress.

➤ What are the different types of stress and what do they entail?

By looking at the different categories of stress, you can easily identify the category that is most likely to affect you. This will help you be more prepared in avoiding or dealing with the stress.

Basically, stress is classified into four main categories and they include the following:

Eustress

This is one type of stress that is actually not bad. It is commonly referred to as "good or positive stress". It normally has a positive impact on an individual and can get one excited about life for a period of time. Eustress is normally short-term. This type of stress comes during specific events and may go away once these events are over.

This is a type of curative stress and may occur prior to physical activities that require high performance such as sports to. For instance, an athlete may experience this kind of stress right before a race. This may actually work towards motivating the athlete to perform very well in their race. Eustress may also occur during instances when creativity is required. For instance, a writer may experience this kind of stress when faced by a major writing project. This will help them get the creativity and motivation required to complete the project successfully.

Eustress may also occur when one is enthusiastic about some things. This kind of stress can actually help one to sum up their energies and give their best effort in trying to achieve something. The most important thing though is to keep this stress in check to avoid being overwhelmed by it. In addition, it only occurs for a short period of time and may actually give one a false sense of contentment that maybe confused for real happiness.

Research shows that people are capable of experiencing eustress over long period of time. This can ensure that the individual lives a very content and fulfilling life. The key is to find out what brings out that feeling of excitement in you. For instance, if painting gives you that thrill, consider doing this more often.

Eustress can motivate and encourage you to give your best performance in an event or task.

Distress

Unlike eustress, distress is negative stress that has bad impacts on a person's body and mind. It may be brought about by changes in life. For instance, if a wealthy person suddenly loses their wealth and is forced to adjust to their new status, they are likely to be distressed. Having to adjust to a new lifestyle or routine maybe overwhelming to the point of getting one stressed. The loss of a loved one may also cause this type of stress. Distress normally brings about feelings of discomfort. It also brings the fear of the unknown. Uncertainty about what will happen in the future and the effect it may have on an individual.

Distress can be further classified into two main categories. These are acute and chronic. Acute distress normally occurs over short periods of time. This kind of stress may be mild or very serious. However, despite its intensity, it is bound to disappear just as fast as it appeared. For instance, a bad incident may get someone very stressed out. However, as soon as the incident is resolved, the stress is likely to go away.

On the other hand, chronic pain usually occurs over a long period of time. It may be intense or not. For instance, terminal instance may bring about chronic stress. A person may be concerned about their wellbeing. They may also be worried about the effects of the illness. This is may bring around some stress for a long period of time. Chronic pain normally occurs if a person doesn't find a way to manage it. It also occurs in instances where it is not possible to get rid of the stressor.

Chronis stress is one of the most serious types of stress. It can have very serious negative impacts on person's health. It can bring about mental problems such as anxiety and depressions. It may also bring about stress related illnesses. In case a person is ill, the stress may actually make their illness much worse.

Distress is negative stress that can affect a person for a short or long period of time.

Hyperstress

When a person is pushed beyond their limits, they are likely to suffer from hyperstress. Every individual has a maximum level of stress that they can handle. Trying to push this person beyond this level will make them breakdown. Many professionals normally suffer from this type of stress. For instance, if one is overworked and unable to get enough stress they will breakdown. It can also happen when one is overloaded with a lot of tasks to do. Panicking about their ability to handle the assignment and complete it on time will definitely become a stressor.

Hyperstress may also occur when one is overwhelmed by many responsibilities at the same time. For instance, if someone who is looking for a job finds out that they are pregnant, this can be stressful. This is because; they are faced by two huge responsibilities that bring a lot of uncertainties about the future.

One of the main symptoms of hyperstress is increased irritability. A person is likely to have a strong emotional reaction even to very little things. For instance, an executive experiencing this kind of stress is likely to yell a lot and even fire any juniors who make the slightest mistakes like spilling coffee or even just a simple grammatical or mathematical error.

Hyperstress is commonly referred to as "being stressed out". This is a phrase that describes the condition of having to deal with more than you can handle.

Hypostress

Many people don't know this but boredom can actually bring about stress. In hyperstress, individuals are stressed by having too much to deal with. On the other hand, in hypostress, individuals are normally stressed by having nothing to do. This kind of stress is likely to occur to people who are unemployed and unable to find a job. This is because they may have nothing that even motivates them to wake up in the morning. They may also have a lot of free time on their hands with no idea on how o spend this.

This kind of stress may also occur to people who lack challenges. For instance, it may occur to someone who is tired of having a routine at work. This person may require new challenges that get them excited and keep them busy. This may happen to young executives who rise up the corporate ladder so fast and then end up hitting a flat line at the end of their careers at a young age. Being bored or having nothing to do can also be stressful to an individual.

CHAPTER 3

AN OVERVIEW OF THE FACTORS
THAT CAUSE STRESS

Synopsis

In this chapter, we look at the factors that bring about stress in different people. We will also look at some of the situations that can make one stressed out.

➢ Is stress normally caused by specific factors?

➢ What avoidable situations are likely to be getting you stressed?

Many people are stressed out unnecessarily. They find themselves in stressful situations that are actually avoidable. If you can identify your stressors, you can learn how to manage your stress.

Life events

There are so many things that can happen in life to get someone stressed out. For instance, loss of employment may be stressful. Other events that can be stressors include, a divorce, death, health problems, being a victim of a crime, sexual frustration, and new distressful environments such as a new job, school or even going to hail.

Money is another big factor that can bring about stress. It can be stressful looking for money, losing money, not having it, owing it or even investing it. Verbal or physical confrontations may also cause stress.

Life events such as the death of a loved one can be very stressful

Relationship problems

It is very easy to be stressed when you are in a relationship that is not working out. For instance, an abusive relationship may easily take a tool on the physical and mental health of an individual hence making them stressed.

Fights whether minor or major can also be stressful. Relationship problems don't just affect romantic relationships.

An estranged relationship between a father and his children may also cause problems. Friendships can also bring about stress.

Perceived or real threats

Any kind of threat can be stressful. Sometimes these threats may be real whereas in other circumstances they may simply be perceived. Some of these threats include financial threats, physical threats, verbal threats or even social threats. These can be stressful to an individual especially if they feel like they have no way of eliminating the threat. However, once the threat is eliminated, the stress may disappear.

Any type of threat whether physical or verbal can bring about stress.

Job stress

This is a very common type of stress. Work can be overwhelming at times. One of the main causes of job stress is work overloads. If employees are unable to handle their workloads then this can get them stressed. Another cause is, poor working environments.

Hostile workplaces where one doesn't get along with other employees or with the boss can also be stressful. Employees who feel undervalued and underpaid can also easily suffer from stress. Work that alienates one from friends and family may also be very stressful.

Too much work can or bad working environments can cause stress.

Change

Change can also be very stressful. For example, moving to a new place can be very stressful. Research also shows that most teenagers are normally stressed by changing schools. Changes such as having a new baby can also be stressful.

Fear

Fear is another factor that can be stressful. It may be any kind of fear. For instance, it may be serious such as the fear of death. It may also be the fear of a person. In other cases, it can also be fear of the unknown. For instance, a person who is considering resigning from their job maybe stressed over their future. Thinking about whether things will work out or not can eliminate peace in one's mind.

Uncertainty

Not knowing what awaits us in future can be very stressful. This may be triggered by an event. For instance, the death of a loved one brings about the fear of having to face life without the departed person. On the other hand, uncertainty may not be brought by events. For instance, some women over thirty years old may get stressed out if they don't have children or are unmarried. Not knowing if they will ever have a family can be a stressor.

Actual Reality versus perceived reality

There are times when people disassociate themselves from reality. They fail to accept their present circumstances and prefer to live the kind of life that they believe they ought to be living. For instance, someone who doesn't have adequate finances may decide to live a lavish lifestyle. This can be very stressful especially if they fail to find the money to support this lifestyle that they want.

Unfulfilled expectations or dreams

Frustration due to unfulfilled expectations can be very stressful. For instance, people who fail to realize their career goals, often tend to get very stressful. A business opportunity that fails to bear fruits can also be very difficult to handle.

Young people also get stressed when they fail to achieve their dreams, For instance, the inability to get admitted to a "dream college" maybe veryn difficult for someone to handle. Stress mostly occurs especially when an individual has very high expectations.

Not eating well

You can actually get stressed if you don't eat a good healthy balanced diet. In addition, not paying attention to what you eat can bring you stress due to weight problems or diet related illnesses. There are also foods that are good for managing stress. Not having these foods in your diet can work against you by alleviating your stress levels.

Eating too much because of stress can give you weight problems.

Individual personalities

There are some personalities that can get someone very stressed. For instance, people who are unable to defend themselves, are likely to keep getting frustrated by others without speaking up. This brings about pent up anger that can be stressful. There are also people who try so much to please everyone. When they fail to do this, they may end up being stressed.

Inadequate rest

Getting enough rest keeps the mind healthy and refreshed. On the other hand, inadequate rest can be very stressful. All bodies are designed to balance between being active and then getting some rest. If you keep pushing yourself without taking a break, you will be stressed. You may also get stressed if you don't get enough sleep. It doesn't matter if you are out having fun or working, you need to get enough sleep so as to be adequately rested.

Illnesses or pain

Sickness can be a cause of stress. For instance, people who are terminally ill may be stressed out. The idea of dying or pain and suffering can overwhelm any individual. Pain especially if it's chronic can be very stressful. Nobody wants to live their lives being constantly in pain and discomfort.

Stress can make you sick. One of the most common symptoms of stress is constant coughs.

CHAPTER 4

AN OVERVIEW OF THE EFFECTS OF STRESS

Synopsis

Stress has a number of effects on a person's body. These effects may be physical, emotional, behavioural or even mental. In this chapter, we look at some of these effects.

➤ How will stress affect your body?

➤ How will it affect how you live and relate with others?

➤ How will stress affect your mind?

Stress usually has both positive and negative effects. Positive effects are good but you have to watch out for the

 negative effects since they can be dangerous to the point of being life threatening.

Health Problems

Stress can greatly affect your health. This commonly happens when stress levels get out of hand. There are a number of health problems that are normally directly linked to stress. Acute or chronic pains can be brought about by stress. One of the most common pains is headaches. A person maybe having severe headaches that cause isn't indefinable. These headaches may be acute of even chronic.

Another common pain is chest pain. Someone may experience a tightening in the chest that can be painful. There are also people who experience a sharp pain in the stomach. All these pains can't be treated by medicine.

Medication may just offer a temporary relief. To get rid of the pain, it is important to move away from the stressor. Stress may also make pain from other illnesses feel much worse. For instance, a stressed cancer patient may easily experience very severe pains.

Stress can also bring about very serious health problems such as heart diseases. It can also affect how the heart functions. For instance, sudden bad news can cause a heart attack. This shows that the person was subjected to high stress levels that their bodies couldn't handle. Living in constant stress can also bring about heart problems.

Stress can also bring about obesity. There are people who like to eat a lot whenever they are stressed up. There are others who turn to their "comfort foods" which in most cases may be junk food. This can bring about rapid weight gain. On the other hand, there are people who experience lack of appetite. They may start skipping meals or eating less. This deprives the body of essential nutrients and may bring about diet deficiency illnesses. It also weakens the body's immunity system making one very susceptible to becoming sick. It also minimizes their ability to fight infections.

Digestive problems may also be easily experienced. A person may start feeling constipated. Other people start having diarrhoea. If the stressor is not removed, the person will not get rid of these symptoms easily.

Stress causes insomnia. Every person needs to get adequate sleep so as to keep their bodies healthy and functioning well. Lack of sleep can bring about more health problems.

In addition, it will inhibit a person's abilities to live normally and continue with their daily routines. On the other hand, there are people who start sleeping a lot when they are stressed. They even have trouble keeping their eyes open even at work or school. This person will feel fatigue and sleepy at all times.

One of the most serious effects of stress is depression. This can greatly affect the quality of a person's life. They will feel alienated from others and may even start isolating themselves. This will definitely have a very negative impact on their relationships. A person may also start experiencing the feeling of hopelessness. They may give up on life. This is very dangerous. Statistics show that the major cause of suicide is depression.

Stress also causes problems with the blood pressure. It can make this go really up or down. In addition, people who have had any previous problems with blood pressure can get serious complications due to stress. Any stressful event can make their blood pressure go up to levels that can be dangerous.

Stress also brings about skin problems. It can bring about acne. A person's skin will also start looking unhealthy and lose its natural glow. People who are stressed tend to look almost ten years older than they actually are. Their skin naturally loses that young fresh look.

Stress can have very serious negative effects on your health.

Psychological Effects

Stress can actually make a person lose their sense of self-worth. They start feeling that they are not equal to others. They may even feel like life has been cruel to them and that maybe they deserve. For instance, a person who has a problem finding a job may easily be stressed. This can happen especially if they see that everyone around them seems to be succeeding in their careers. They may start thinking that they do lack something that others have. They may also start feeling like they will never be able to achieve their goals. Stress can actually lower a person's self-esteem.

Stress can make a person feel very negative about life. This person will be unable to think positively. They may lose interest in their dreams or the pursuit of these dreams. Such a person may start withdrawing from others. They may also start giving up on things that they used to enjoy doing. For instance, an artist may suddenly lose interest in art. They will adapt the "what's the point" attitude. This means that everything seems to have lost meaning to them.

Stress can make someone very negative about life.

Behavioural Effects

Most people turn to drugs and alcohol when they are stressed. They normally use this as an escapism strategy. A person may start drinking to avoid dealing with stress at home or at work. They may also turn to drugs so as to get a quick relief from their stress. However, this relief is normally very temporary. Once the effects of the alcohol or drugs fade away, the person will again start feeling the stress. This is why it is better to find permanent stress relief that an escapism strategy of not dealing with your stress.

Stress can cause alcohol or drug abuse.

A person may also start acting irrational. This is a common phenomenon that some people refer as to "one not acting themselves". They will make rush decisions that seem completely out of character. The decisions they make may not be bad. They may seem good but in actual sense they may have negative repercussions.

For instance, a person may suddenly decide to buy a flashy new sports car despite their current financial problems. On the other hand, some of the irrational decisions may be dangerous. For instance a person may start turning to violence to resolve their issues. They may also quit their jobs and start living recklessly.

Irritability is also another behavioural change that can be brought about by stress. A person may start an argument even over very minor issues. They may also seem overly frustrated over things that aren't that serious. For instance, a father may start yelling at his kids for making even slightest mistakes such as breaking a cup. People also tend to be very quick tempered. They are likely to have a strong emotional response to everything. Trying to make a joke or prank this person can easily get you a very major tongue lashing. People also become violent. They may get into physical fights with the slightest provocation whether actual or perceived.

A stressed person may get into a fight even with little or no provocation at all.

Cognitive Effects

One of the most common cognitive effects of stress is memory loss. A stressed person can easily become forgetful. They will make plans and completely forget about them. An employee may forget his assignments completely. A spouse may forget important dates such as anniversaries. Forgetfulness may be temporary or long-term.

People also tend to have a lapse in memory. They may not be able to remember things that they said or did not long ago. This simply happens due to the minds inability to concentrate on anything else apart from the stressor.

Another common effect is inability to concentrate on anything. This can greatly hinder a person's performance in a number of areas. They may be unable to concentrate at work and therefore end up losing their jobs. They may also be unable to concentrate in school and therefore start performing very poorly.

A person may not be able to perform simple tasks that they use to enjoy. They may not even be able to sit still and watch their favourite movie or listen to music. Their only preoccupation is the stressful event or situation.

A stressed person may also have low sex drive. They will withdraw from all forms of intimacy be it sexual or even emotional. Stress can easily tear apart a relationship due to the lack of intimacy between the couple.

Stress can make one lose interest in any form of intimacy particularly sex.

Effects of Positive Stress

As earlier on discussed in the eBook, there is positive stress. This is what is referred to as Eustress. The effects of this type of stress are usually good. They can help someone be more creative or gain the necessary energy and motivation to perform very well in any given task

CHAPTER 5

AN OVERVIEW OF HOW TO ABOLISH STRESS

Synopsis

If you are feeling stressed right now and it doesn't seem like things will get better, you need to realize that you can take control of your situation. In this chapter, you get to learn that it actually is possible to abolish stress from your life.

➢ How can you get rid of stress in your life?

You need to act now. You don't have to go through your life being stressed out. Stress will keep you from enjoying your life. It will also keep you from pursuing your goals. Taking the steps to abolish stress from your life is the first step towards living a more fulfilling life.

Establish and Eliminate the Source of Your Stress

You have to establish what is stressing you. Find out what makes you feel the most overwhelmed. You should also try and find out when the stress started. This can enable you to identify the cause of the stress. For instance, if you started feeling stressed out when you moved in a house with someone else, you may want to examine this since it may be your stressor. Getting rid of your stressor may be the most effective way of getting rid of your stress.

Let someone else know what you are going through

Talking to someone doesn't necessarily mean going for therapy, you can confide in anyone who you trust. For example, if you find that your schoolwork is overwhelming you, you can talk to a teacher or school counsellor or even your parent. You can also talk to your friends. It doesn't mean that you need advise so as to feel better. Just letting it out and talking about your issues can be very good for you.

Talking to a friend about what is stressing you can be very helpful.

Time management

If you learn how to manage your time well, you can easily learn how to get rid of stress. Sometimes, we may have a manageable workload that becomes overwhelming due to poor time management. You may find some stress relief by simply learning how to plan your time well. Try and start your day by making a plan with actual time frames. If you have to be at work or school by 8 o'clock, give yourself ample time to make this. If you start running around some minutes to 8, you will find yourself very stressed out. Time management is a great stress reliever.

Don't ignore your stress

Your body will alert you when you are stressed out. You will notice some signs of being overwhelmed. Your behavioural changes can also alert you of stress. The worst thing that you can do is to ignore your stress. If you feel that your work is stressing you, you can't just ignore this and keep pushing yourself. You will only do more harm to your mind and body. You have to act now!

Avoid stressful situations

If you know that certain events or places normally get you stressed, you should then avoid them. In the next chapter, you will learn about how to do this. However, if you study the factors that were discussed in chapter 3 as the causes of stress, you can find out which ones are likely to affect you and then learn how to stay away from them.

Take a break

You need to take a break from time to time. If you find yourself in a stressful situation and are unable to get rid of the cause of stress, then you need to get away. If your work is becoming stressful, you don't have to quit.

Maybe just taking a simple break will do you good. Getting away doesn't just mean going on vacation or travelling far, you can get some time alone at home to relax. If you find yourself in a room with a person that stresses you, maybe you can get out of the room and away from your stressor.

Taking a break or going away on vacation can help you get rid of stress.

Set realistic goals and learn to celebrate your successes

Everyone has some goals in life; they could be personal or even career goals. It is common to find someone setting their goals based on other people's expectations or successes.

You may want to be a doctor just because that's what your father wants for you. You may also want to be a doctor because your friend is a doctor. This can be frustrating especially if you don't succeed. You ought to learn how to set realistic goals and do what you enjoy. You should also appreciate yourself and your accomplishments.

Get some help

It is human nature to work together. It's not good to try and do everything yourself. Sometimes, everyone needs some help .If you feel overwhelmed, you should ask a friend or relative to help you out. For instance, if you have kids, a job and school to manage all at the same time, this can be overwhelming.

However, you can ask someone to watch your kids for an hour or two so that you can take a break. Many people think asking for help is a sign of weakness, however this isn't true. Asking for help is the smart thing to do to keep yourself from being overwhelmed by all your responsibilities.

If you feel overwhelmed whether at work, school or even at home, you should ask someone else to help you out.

Try not to multi-task

Sometimes trying to carry out several tasks at the same time can be very stressful. For instance, trying to do an assignment, cook a meal and feed the baby all at the same time can be very stressful. However, if you carry out this tasks one at a time, you may be able to complete them without feeling overwhelmed.

Learn how to relax

You don't have to be busy all the time. Sometimes it's ok to just lying down and so nothing. You can clear your mind and just get away from everything that is stressing you.

You should also find the things that get you relaxed. Some people relax by watching a movie, playing a game, listening to music, reading a good book, hanging out with friends or even cooking. You have to identify what works for you .Do this often especially when you are feeling overwhelming or stressed out.

Taking some time to just sit down and relax can help you avoid getting stressed out.

Get professional help

If you feel stressed out, you may consider talking to someone. This is especially important if you have been having this feeling for a period of time. Getting professional help can help you get back to living your life normally. It is never good to keep your negative feelings or emotions bottled up. This will just get you more stressed. Finding release by talking to a professional may be very helpful.

Help others

It is true that helping others can actually help you alleviate stress. You will feel good about yourself also. In addition, it will also help you take your mind off the cause of your stress. In addition, making a change in someone else's life will give you the sense of self worth and make you feel better about yourself.

You can volunteer at a home or a church sometimes. This can also be a great way to help people. There are so many organizations that need help such as feeding the homeless.

Positive thinking

You need to get rid of negative thoughts that may be putting you down. Learn to adapt a positive mind frame and change your outlook on life. In addition, having a positive attitude will also help improve the quality of your life and therefore get rid of some of your stresses. Sometimes, the stress is all in our mind, change your thoughts and you get rid of it. You can try using positive affirmations to get you thinking positively.

Socialize and stop isolating yourself

It is common to want to isolate yourself from others especially when you feel like you are stressed out. However, you can't do this. You need to be around people. A good support system will help you abolish stress from your life. It's good to get some alone time but it's never good to isolate yourself from others.

To avoid stress, avoid isolating yourself from others. Socializing is highly advisable.

Be happy

Did you know that you can actually decide to be happy no matter what you are going through? Just make a conscious decision to be happy and don't let anything put you down. This will help you focus your life on more positive things. It will also get you a better outlook on life. It is said that you can learn how to happy by learning how to appreciate what you have instead of focusing on what you don't have.

Make up your mind today and decide to be happy. This is a great way of avoiding stress.

Use relation techniques

You can try out meditation to help you clear your mind. This is a great way of taking a break from the stresses of your life without even needing to travel. Meditation will also teach you discipline. This will help you every time you start feeling stressed. Yoga also helps in meditating and channelling positive vibes through the mind and the body.

Exercises and eat healthy

This is a great and important way to help you abolish stress from your life. Exercising frequently can help to keep your body and mind healthy. You don't have to go to the gym; you can just take a nice relaxing walk to get you some exercise. A good well balanced diet can also go a long way in helping you abolish stress from your life.

Get adequate sleep

It is recommended to get at least six hours of sleep each night. This will help you in relaxing your mind and body. Going for days without sleep will get you overwhelmed by life.

CHAPTER 6

AN OVERVIEW OF HOW TO AVOID
GETTING STRESSED

Synopsis

There is a common saying that says "Prevention is better than cure". In this chapter, we look at some of things that one can do so as to avoid being stressed.

➢ How can one live a stress-free life?

➢ Is it really possible to avoid stress?

You can manage to live life free of stress. You only need to learn how to stay away from the factors that cause stress.

Some Strategies

Talking it out

When you talk to someone about your problems, you will feel much better. This is highly recommended as opposed to keeping your emotions all bottled up. You should find a good friend or any other person who is ready to hear you out and confide in them.

However, you need to be careful about the people you choose to confide in. There are people that you can never trust with your secrets since they may use them against you. In addition, there are people who you may confide in only to have them discourage you and add you more stress.

Crying can also be very helpful. Sometimes people try to keep their emotions bottled up inside them for fear of showing emotion that may be perceived as a sign of weakness. However, sometimes if you feel like crying, just do it .You can do it behind closed doors if you don't want anyone to see you. Crying is a good way to relieve stress. It also really helps in the grieving process.

There are also instances where it is advisable to seek professional help. For instance, if you go through a traumatic experience like being a crime victim, you have to talk to a therapist. Keeping this experience to yourself can cause you chronic stress. You may end up spending your life being held hostage by the memories of this traumatic experience. This type of stress is commonly referred to as, post traumatic stress disorder. It is very dangerous and can have very serious impacts on a person's life.

Yoga and mediation

Yoga can really help you in avoiding stress. Meditation will help you learn how to control your mind. You will learn how to calm your mind and get some inner peace. This will help you in preventing getting overwhelmed by anything that can be described as being stressful. You can join a yoga class or alternatively do yoga on your own. Just go online and download some yoga poses. Then try this out at home. Remember, you have to be committed. Find a nice quiet room and set aside enough time for your yoga and meditations. If possible, do this at least once each day.

Yoga can help in relaxing the mind and abolishing stress

Humour

Everyone needs to laugh. A good sense of humour goes a long way in helping one avoid stress. You need to learn how not to take things too serious. It is also good to laugh how to learn yourself. You can read humorous articles or watch comedies to lighten up your mood. This will help you take your mind off everything else and just relax. Learning how to laugh a lot can really help you in getting rid of stress.

You should also try and stay away from people who are gloomy all the time. There are people who you can't even laugh around. This negative energy will only make it worse for you. You will be more stressed by socializing with such people. For instance, if you are mourning, you don't have to stay with other mourners all the time. This will keep your mind focused on the death of the person. You can take a break and just get away with your friend. Go somewhere and have a cup of coffee way from the mourning.

Music and dancing

Good music has the ability to lighten up even the darkest days. It can bring one inner peace and calmness. For instance after a long day at work, take some time and listen to soft soothing music. You will feel the pressures of the day washing away. Listening to music or dancing can help you stay healthy physically and mentally.

You don't have to go out in the club to have some good fun. Just listening to music at home and dancing alone can be very helpful. In some work environment, it is allowed to listen to music especially during the breaks. This is a great way to take a break from your busy work schedule and just relax for a while.

Listening to music and dancing can help you avoid getting stressed out.

Know your limitations

Everyone wants to maximize on their full potential. However, it is vital to know your limitations. You have to know what your mind and body can comfortably handle. For instance, at work, don't take up too many assignments that may affect you. Sometimes, you may be motivated by the chance to make money or even get a good appraisal. However, it is said that if you stress yourself so as to make money this is a waste. This is because you may just end up using all the money you made in hospital looking for treatment for the stress related illnesses.

Positive attitude

You need to learn how to have a positive outlook of life. Being negative all the time will just get you stressed. Even when you are going through tough situations, you have to keep reminding yourself that this is temporary. Use affirmations to remind yourself that you have the strength and ability to get through the toughest times. A defeated attitude will not only affect the quality of your life but also keep you stressed.

Get rid of your stressors

There are times when one may know their potential stressors but still not get away. For example, if you are in a relationship that is not working out. This may be a potential stressor for you. You can choose to get out of the relationship or find a way to make it work. If you are currently stressed, you should try and establish where the stress is originating from. You should then try and get rid of the cause.

You should also avoid people or places that normally get you stressed. For instance, there are friends who can really put you down .This are people who flaunt their successes and constantly remind you of your own failures. You should stay away from such people. If a place like a bank that normally has very long queues stresses you out, find a way of doing your banking without having to stand in line for so long. You can find away to get away from things that get you stressed out. This is one of the best ways to avoid or get rid of stress.

Learn to manage your time

There are times when people get stressed, not because they have too much workload but because they are unable to manage their times. You should pan your time well. Leave room for work and rest equally. You should also try as much possible to work with only realistic goals. Set your goals and a time frame and then work towards achieving this.

You should also learn how to do things in good time. Last minute rushes tend to be very stressful. This is because of the fear of missing a target or just the fact that one has too much to do within a very short period of time. For instance, if you have an exam in one month's time, start studying in advance. Waiting until the last week to start getting ready can be very stressful. You may realize that you have so many topics to cover in just one week. Panic will get you stressed. Trying to read day and night to cover all topics will also get you overwhelmed. It is better to get ready for the four weeks so that you avoid that stressful last minute rush.

Take a break

Everyone needs a good break from time to time. It could be a break from school, work or even home. Time away can help clear the mind and avoid potential stress. It can also provide relief for people who are stressed. A good vacation can also be very helpful for everyone. It gives people time to relax their bodies and minds.

Taking a break between tasks can also be very helpful. For instance, it is not advisable to study for four hours straight. This can get you very stressed especially if you are covering new information. You can take a ten minutes break after two hours. This will help you relax your mind for a little while and also give you strength and freshness to go through the remaining two hours.

You can also take a break from your relationships. For instance, if you and

your girlfriend or boyfriends are in constant disagreements, getting some time away from each other can be helpful. It can help you figure out whether or not you want to be together. It can also help you get some time to relax your mind.

Taking a break from a stressful relationship can help you get rid of stress.

Exercising and eating a good diet

A good workout can also help you avoid stress. You can go to the gym or simply take a walk. Exercising is good not just for the mind but also for the body. You should also avoid junk food and eat healthy. A good diet will really help you in avoiding stress. Like exercising, it is beneficial both to the mind and the body.

Breathing exercises can also be very beneficial in getting rid of stress. You can easily do this from any given locations. For instance, when at work, if you start feeling overwhelmed, take a few minutes and take some deep breathes. This can help calm your mind and gain focus.

Other ways of avoiding stress include, not worrying about things that can't be changed. There are so many people who get stressed over things that they actually have no control over. For instance, if you aren't as tall you would like to be, this isn't something to worry about. There is nothing you can do about it so juts accept it and try and move on.

You should also learn how to let go of the past. There are people who live very stressful lives because they refuse to let go of their past. They keep reliving their mistakes and wallowing in unnecessary misery. If you made bad financial decisions, love from them and move them back. Thinking about this constantly is really not going to help you in any way.

Regular exercising can help you avoid stress.

Wrapping up

To abolish stress is not hard. It only requires a few steps. You don't have to live your life constantly feeling stressed and unhappy. This will ruin your life. It will keep you from excelling in your responsibilities at work, school or even at home.

It will also greatly affect how you relate with others. Your relationships will be strained or even totally ruined. Stress can also get you depressed and bring about suicidal thoughts. It may make you give up on your life and the pursuit of your dreams. This will definitely affect the quality of your life and also of those who depend on you.

Identify the causes of stress

You can learn how to identify factors that may causes you stress. This will help you in learning how to avoid it. Preventing stress is much more effective that waiting till you get overwhelmed to do something about it. Doing very simple things to avoid the stress may be beneficial to you. It will also save you some time and money that you may otherwise have to spend to get rid of stress.

Listen to your body

You body will alert you when your stress levels start getting out of hand. This may be in form of illnesses or just psychological changes. It is very important that you know the stress symptoms. It is then important that you listen to your these symptoms. You have to acknowledge that you have a problem that needs to be addressed.

Do something about it

Once you identify the stress symptoms, you have to be willing to do something about this. You should never accept the stress as just part of your life. This is something that has so many negative impacts on you. You have to do something about it as soon as possible.

Take charge of your life today and get rid of stress from your life. Successfully doing this will practically give you a new lease on life. You will learn how to be more relaxed and learn how to enjoy your life. You may also get rid of some of your health problems simply by abolishing stress from your life.

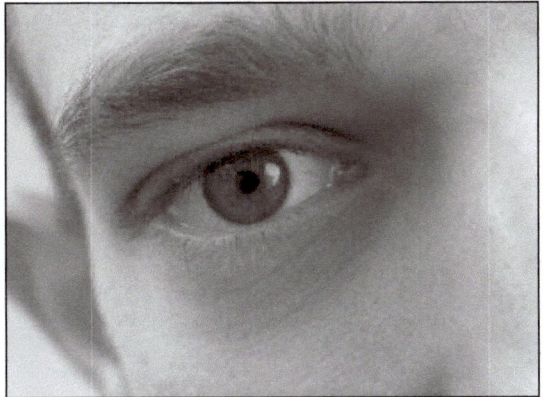

Printed by Libri Plureos GmbH in Hamburg, Germany